CONCRETE SPIRIT

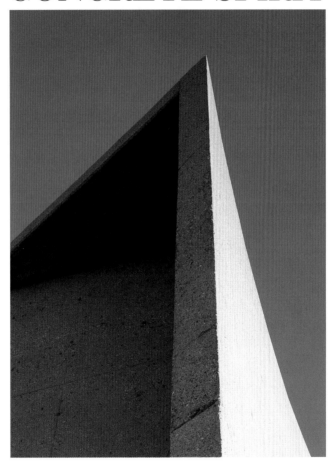

The Architecture *of*
Ralph Allen

To my wife Joyce for her support, and to the memory of my parents,
Oral and Lottie Allen, who encouraged me to get an education.

CONCRETE SPIRIT

The Architecture *of* Ralph Allen

Rockport Publishers
Rockport, Massachusetts

First published in the United States of America by:
Rockport Publishers, Inc.
146 Granite Street
Rockport, Massachusetts 01966
Telephone: 508-546-9590
Fax: 508-546-7141

Distributed to the book trade and art trade in the U.S. by:
The A.I.A. Press
1735 New York Avenue
Washington, D.C. 20006
Telephone: 800-365-ARCH
Fax: 800-678-7102

Other distribution by:
Rockport Publishers, Inc.
Rockport, Massachusetts 01966

ISBN 1-56496-219-9
10 9 8 7 6 5 4 3 2 1

Page 2: Century High School. Photo by Per Volquartz
Page 6: Orange County Law Library. Photo by Julius Shulman

Printed in Singapore

Graphic Design: Lucas H. Guerra / Argus Visual Communication, Boston

Contents

Foreword

During the course of nearly 60 years as an architectural photographer, I've had the opportunity to view close up the work of hundreds of architects. This experience has provided me with an insight into how they work, and what makes an architect run!

Since my first assignment for Ralph Allen, the Orange County Law Library in 1972, I came upon the conclusion that the success of an architect is frequently belabored by critics and the so-called authorities on architecture. To me, the identification of design success is predicated upon the structure's admittance and satisfaction of the client's various needs.

The work of Ralph Allen to this day reflects his massive concern for integrity and respect of and for the client's program. This is not a simple task in these days fraught with tricks, devious detours, and false fronts, dedicated to filling the pages of the architectural press.

Hats off to Ralph Allen! He and his creatively efficient staff continue to embellish our environment with sound structures, somehow avoiding the ensnaring temptations to follow the false Messiahs of architecture.

Julius Shulman
Los Angeles, California

Introduction

Ralph Allen's architectural philosophy has evolved from his concern for the client and the users, particularly how they will perceive the buildings he designs. His philosophy consists of keeping the work within budget, using energy-conserving elements wherever possible, while solving unique architectural problems with elegance, form, and proportion. Searching for an appropriate response is the key to his successful design process. He's rarely satisfied with his first solution.

As a practitioner within the Modernist tradition, Allen uses natural shapes, which people relate to, with an intriguing twist. They often find his buildings and their forms so familiar, so comfortable, and so vibrant. Allen's work comes alive through his integration of the built and natural environments. He takes advantage of the space within which the building is sited, and blends the outside environment to create sculptural, bold, and simple forms. He uses these forms and natural shapes to resolve difficult site and programmatic challenges.

Allen's work shows the influence of such International Style architects as Mies van der Rohe and Walter Gropius. By using pure, simple forms that take maximum advantage of shade and shadow, Allen creates memorable architecture with a strong Bauhaus aesthetic. He makes function and an economy of means driving forces in his designs. Effective site planning for efficient utilization of space and appropriate human scale are hallmarks of his architecture.

Throughout his projects, Allen exploits the power of materials, particularly that of concrete, to give his architecture a sense of presence and permanence. The Orange County Law Library in Santa Ana, California, for instance, uses simple planes and strong concrete massing to create the image of strength and power which the law profession signifies. Deep-set windows against planes create interesting shadows and also save energy. The jury that gave the Law Library a design award cited the building for its "sophisticated use of concrete, and strong, handsome massing."

Allen's Fremont Elementary School in Santa Ana was appraised by the National AIA Committee on Architecture for Education as one of the most exemplary educational environments in the country. The basic premise of the school's design was to place the structure on the 2.8-acre site in harmony with the densely populated neighborhood. By recessing the building into the ground with the use of simple, poured-in-place concrete forms, he was able to fit the school into the site while creating a parklike setting above, and improving the building's energy performance. The design's innovative energy features earned it a National Award in the AIA/Owens Corning Energy Conservation Program. "The designers used the building mass time lag to great advantage by shifting the heat gain to a later time in the afternoon," comment the awards jury.

At the Transportation District Maintenance Facility in Anaheim, California, limited space and a limited budget were the driving design forces. The use of low-maintenance, sand-blasted concrete block allowed the architect to create a cost-efficient solution without sacrificing the building's powerful image. Pure forms take advantage of shade and shadow, helping to create airy spaces filled with natural light. The jury that cited this project for a design award noted that it showed how "a talented and experienced designer using simple materials can transform an ordinary and often-overlooked structure to service buses into a handsome, high-quality part of the community. That's what architecture is all about."

Allen has also been influenced by the work of Eero Saarinen, Le Corbusier, and I.M. Pei. Allen is a "form giver." His architecture has evolved into fluid, sculptural pieces of art, utilizing structural shapes that relate to nature in a dignified and coherent way.

For example, at the U.S. Navy Troop Training Facility in Coronado, California, the entire building is conceived as a geometric system of planes, curves, and circular elements, whose exposed concrete and masonry surfaces create a purity of form. Through the various shapes, the building's design relates symbolically to its use as an amphibious training facility. Spatial efficiency was a major factor in this project, therefore, an inventive,

Above: *U.S. Navy Troop Training Facility.* **Left:** *Orange County Law Library.* **Previous Spread:** *Century High School.*
All Drawings by Sergio O'Cadiz

geometrically bold approach to architectural design was taken. Creating a circular volume and dividing classrooms into wedges make the building more space efficient, with rounded, theaterlike sections that are conducive to concentration. When cited for a design award, the jury commented that the training facility "takes a number of similar uses and combines them into an imaginative, enclosed circular volume that is quite exceptional and surprising for a building of its kind."

For the Orange Covenant Church in Orange, California, Allen used simple, basic materials and construction methods in an efficient manner, without sacrificing the project's aesthetics. Taking this approach, along with an emphasis on energy conservation, Allen created a cost-effective project from initial construction to long-term use. Upon entering the church, your attention is drawn to the altar from where the fan-shaped plan unfolds with clean lines. By integrating familiar geometry and sculptural elements in a coherent manner, Allen creates a dramatic visual impact. "The precise abstraction of the church is an example of geometric formulations," noted the design awards jury that cited this project, "which enable the construction of wholeness out of elemental parts."

The influences of Saarinen and Le Corbusier are especially evident in the design of Century High School in Santa Ana. A tight site led Allen to integrate the building into it, and to put the 300 required parking spaces on the roof. The resultant cost savings allowed the design and construction of an amphitheater and the use of high-finish concrete. By using concrete as the major building material, Allen was able to take advantage of its plastic and formal qualities, creating fluid, curving elements combined with simple geometry. The main facade of the building is truly sculpture.

Setting his buildings in a field of space, being conscious of energy consumption, and exploiting the expressive qualities of the materials make Allen's architecture socially relevant and sculptural—a deft blending of function and form, realized through the spirit of concrete.

Century High School

Santa Ana, California

Designed to accommodate 1,800 students, Century High School occupies a 25-acre site bordered by commercial and industrial buildings. This context naturally led to a design that would shelter the building from its noisy, distracting neighborhood. Cast-in-place concrete was the material of choice to enhance the building's thermal performance and to help insulate it from its surroundings.

Placing a parking lot for 300 cars on the building's roof allowed an additional 150,000 square feet to be added for uses such as landscaping and sports fields. The parking helps to submerge the building into the site, hunkering down to shield it from neighboring buildings. The roof-top lot also functions as a heat-sink, absorbing the sun's warmth and reducing the cooling load inside. At the center is a protected courtyard with a circular amphitheater for outside performances, and shading provided by concrete lattice that extends from the roof. These concrete overhangs protect south-facing glass from heat-gain.

The building's most visible feature from the road is the curved concrete facade that appears to float like a spirit. This cantilevered wall has a bush-hammered finish that softens its edges and gives the surface a variegated texture. Concrete is expressed inside the building through the specially designed coffer ceilings.

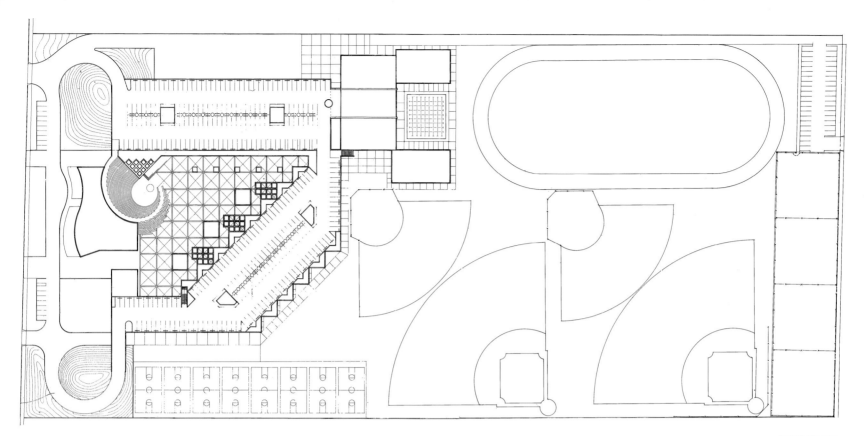

SITE PLAN

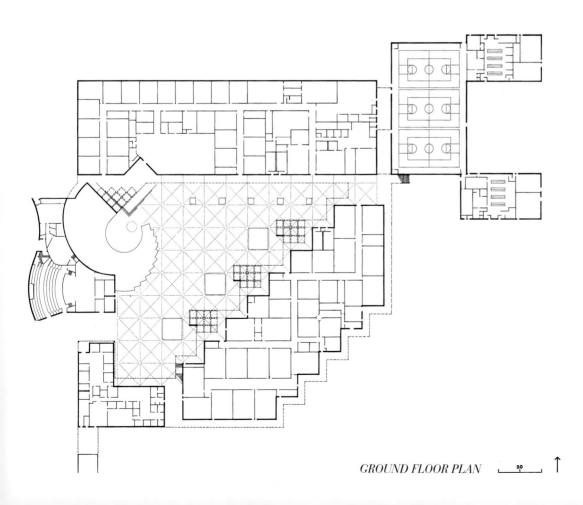

GROUND FLOOR PLAN |—30—| ↑

Previous Spread: *The west wall of the music performance wing appears to be a concrete flag hovering over the landscape. Photo: Harvey Spector.* **Left:** *An aerial view of the school reveals the protected courtyard at its center. Photo: Eagle Aerial Photography.* **Below:** *From the air, the stair/ramp, or "stramp," provides an abstract pattern. Photo: Eagle Aerial Photography*

Above: *The gently sloped ramp of concrete and brick is a sculptural element in the school's large courtyard.*

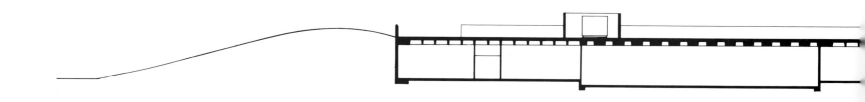

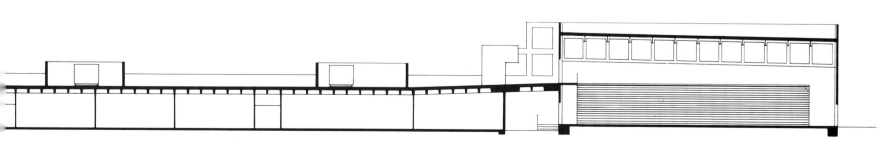

SECTION AT LIBRARY AND GYM   **16**

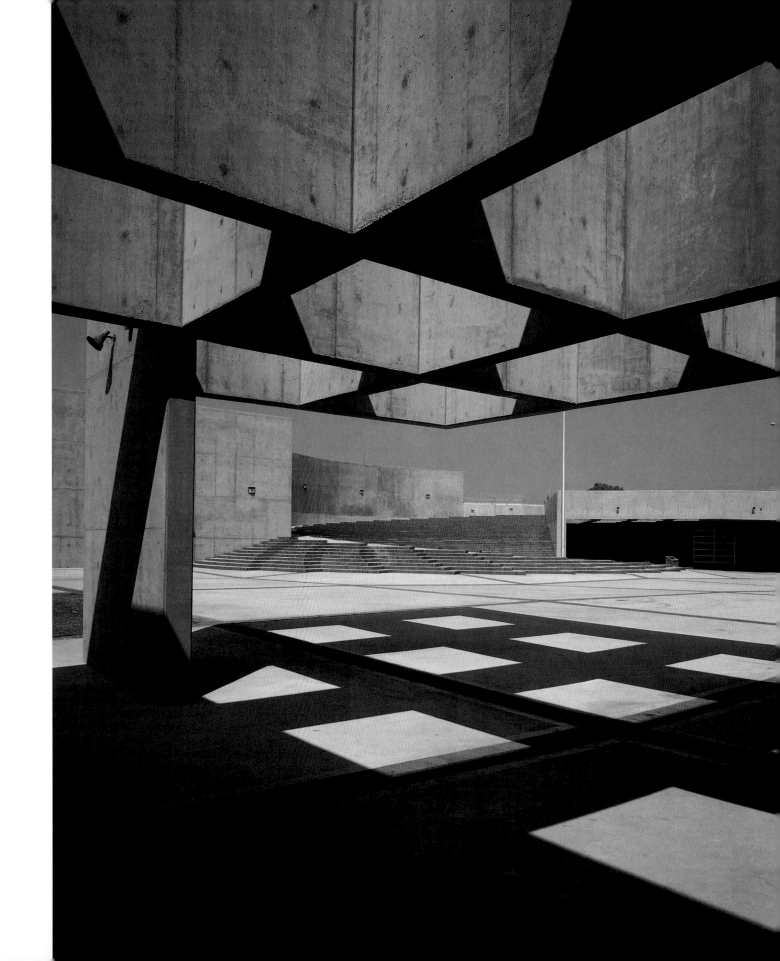

Above: *The school's fern garden is found under one of the many concrete canopies that filter the sunlight.* **Opposite Page:** *The concrete canopies provide shading when the courtyard is used during mid-day. Photos: Per Volquartz*

Right: *The desk in the library is situated near the glass wall overlooking the courtyard.* **Below:** *The interior of the library is distinguished by a concrete waffle-slab ceiling and a specially commissioned mural.* **Opposite Page:** *The waffle-slab ceiling of the library extends outside to provide shading. Photos: Per Volquartz*

Above: *The warm climate of California allows student lockers and lounge areas to be located outside.* **Opposite Page:** *Concrete in the courtyard is left with its natural finish, and is virtually maintenance-free.*

Moffett Elementary School

Lennox, California

High land costs, prevalent vandalism, and a site directly under the approach to Los Angeles airport all contributed to the partial subterranean architecture of this school. To preserve as much open land as possible on the nine-acre site, parking for 100 cars was placed on the building's roof. This decision led to the building's concrete structure, which also accommodates the need to dampen aircraft noise and the client's desire for low-maintenance materials.

The roof consists of 12-inch-thick reinforced concrete, four inches of insulation, and four inches of concrete topping. Earth berming on the building's southwest side, cast-in-place concrete, and a roof structure that serves as a heat sink delay the sun's warmth from entering the building during school hours. A one-way concrete slab and joist system was used for multi-purpose and kindergarten rooms on the north side. For the lobby and library, an exposed ten-foot-square concrete waffle slab gives the ceiling a sculptural quality.

The third structural system used in the 55,000-square-foot school are 12-inch-thick two-way flat slabs with columns on a 30-foot grid, which accommodated the classroom size of 30 x 30 feet. The subterranean perimeter walls are 12 to 15 inches thick and are left with their natural finish. To repel graffiti, the concrete walls were treated with a waterproof sealant.

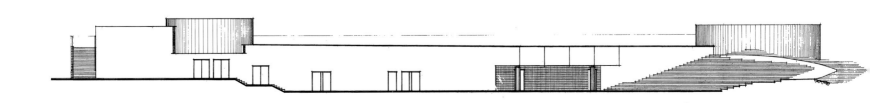

Previous Spread: *From the southwest, the building hunkers into the site, with the entrance marked by the folded concrete plane. Photo: Harvey Spector.* **Left:** *An aerial view of the school is dominated by the rooftop parking lot. Photo: Eagle Aerial Photography*

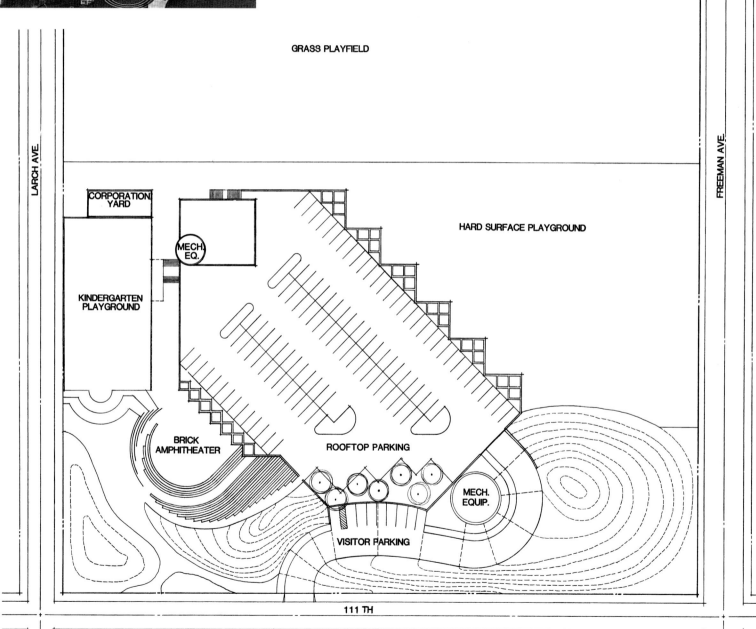

GRASS PLAYFIELD

LARCH AVE.

FREEMAN AVE.

CORPORATION YARD

HARD SURFACE PLAYGROUND

MECH. EQ.

KINDERGARTEN PLAYGROUND

BRICK AMPHITHEATER

ROOFTOP PARKING

MECH. EQUIP.

VISITOR PARKING

111 TH

SITE PLAN

Above: *The amphitheater for school assemblies gently climbs the site, offering access to the rooftop parking lot. Photo: Harvey Spector*

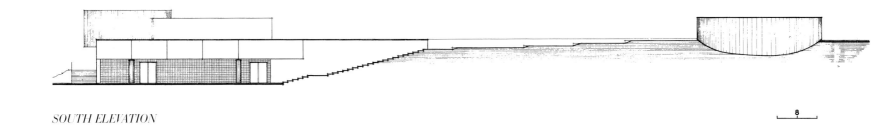

SOUTH ELEVATION

1. Multipurpose Room
2. Platform
3. Play Yard Storage
4. Custodial Storage
5. Shower
6. Handicapped Lift
7. Kiln
8. Restroom
9. Staff Lounge
10. Library
11. Kitchen
12. Staff Workroom
13. Resource Center
14. Teacher's Storage
15. Kindergarten Classroom
16. Instructional Supply Storage
17. Basic Classroom 28 Total

18. Reading Area
19. Speech Lab
20. Special Ed. Classroom 2 Total
21. Principal
22. Clerical
23. Assistant Principal
24. Clerical Machines
25. Timeout Booths
26. Entry Foyer
27. Nurse
28. Conference
29. Counselor
30. Psych. Testing
31. Remedial Labs
32. Computer Lab
33. Textbook Storage

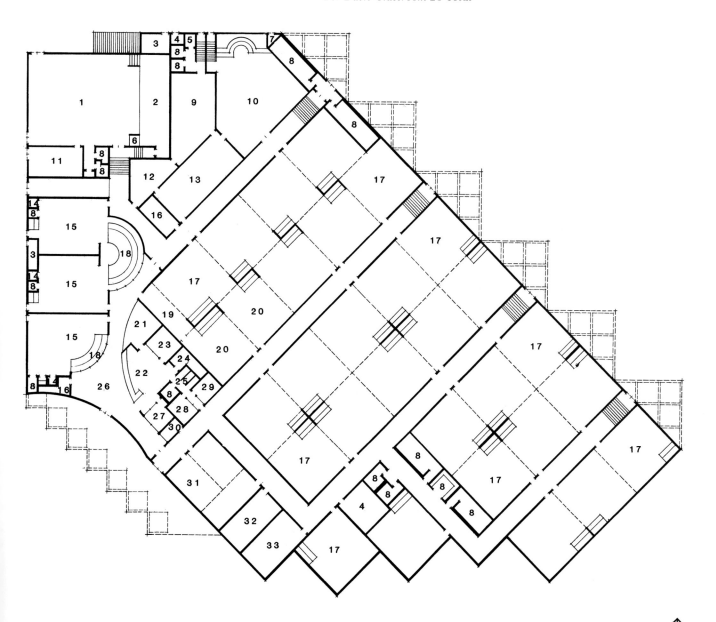

FLOOR PLAN

16

ROOFTOP PARKING

ENTRY FOYER

MULTIPURPOSE

Opposite Page: *The kindergarten play area sports its own concrete climbing structure.*
Below: *The entrance accessed from the brick amphitheater is shaded by a perforated concrete canopy. Photos: Harvey Spector*

Above: *The library features a reading nook illuminated from a glass-block wall.*
Opposite Page: *The school's reception area is distinguished by a concrete coffer ceiling divided into triangular patterns. Photos: Harvey Spector*

Orange Covenant Church

Orange, California

This sanctuary was designed as an addition to an existing facility that lacked a distinctive identity for the church. A major goal in the design was to use the building form to encourage a sense of unification and fellowship in the congregation. In addition to the sanctuary are a foyer, choir room, and a meeting room.

The 7,200-square-foot addition takes the shape of an open semi-circular fan, with the altar as the focal point and curved seating radiating from it. The sanctuary entrance is located to one side of the foyer to allow the congregation to observe other members as they enter. The fan shape is reflected on the exterior by the building's bold curve and a cantilevered, terraced area, which makes the church appear to float. Natural lighting is achieved with ribbon windows on the curved facade, which also open for ventilation. A 78-foot-tall sculptural tower, topped with a cross, suggests a campanile and gives the building an identity on the city skyline.

The exterior is finished with stonecrete, a material that allows shadows to model the building's form. Small stones are embedded into the surface, creating a texture of shadow as the sun rakes across the curved surfaces.

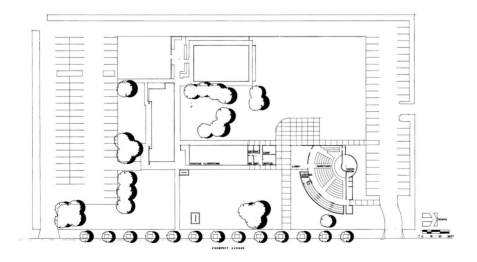

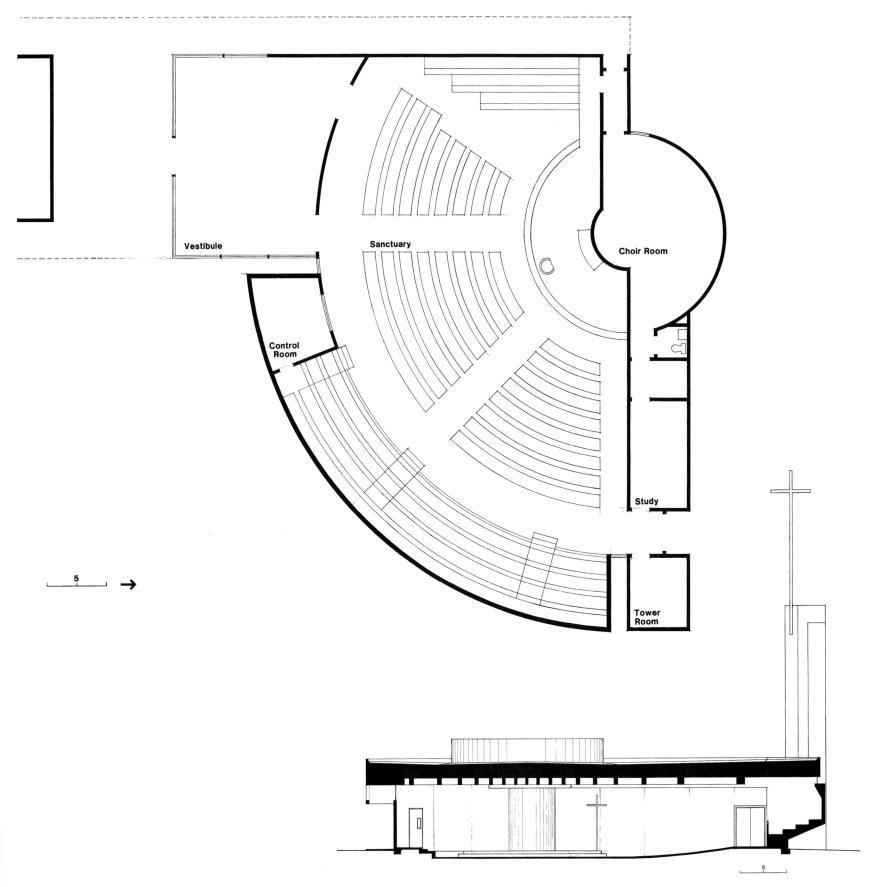

Vestibule

Sanctuary

Choir Room

Control Room

Study

Tower Room

5

5

Previous Spread: *From the southeast, the church appears to float above the site, with the entrance to the left.*
Right: *The church is marked by a sculptural concrete tower at the northeast corner. Photos: Julius Shulman*

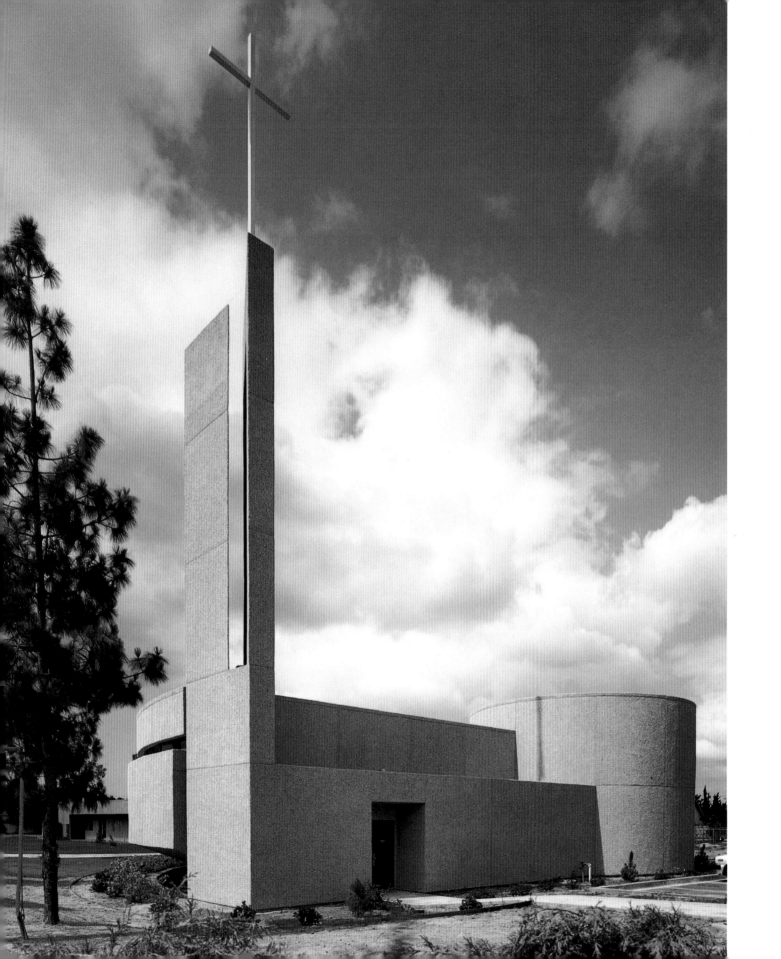

Previous Spread: *The church from the west, with view of the terrace for small outdoor gatherings. Photo: Julius Shulman* Above: *View from the north aisle toward the altar, with choir seating beyond and stained-glass ribbon widows. Photo: Julius Shulman.* Opposite Page: *The sanctuary's roof structure radiates from the altar area, drawing one's eyes to the center.*

Fountain Valley Library

Fountain Valley, California

This 15,000-square-foot library had to meet a variety of sensitive site conditions. The building had to be close to adjacent residential and commercial structures, respond to its civic use, accommodate on-site parking, and relate to a small historical park adjacent to it.

Locating the building to the west end of the site buffered it from nearby residences to the east. The building reaches to the street to welcome pedestrian visitors, while its west elevation relates to the park by creating a theatrical setting. To the north, the library has a civic scale to relate to a nearby government center. Thus, the building sensitively responds in a different, appropriate way to a range of contextual issues.

The plan establishes a procession from the entry, to the charge desk, to the information desk, which gives the visitor a range of choices. Stacks are located under lower ceiling areas with reading nooks, illuminated with natural light under clerestory windows. Other specially designed spaces with reading in mind include lounges, one with a fireplace, and a children's library with a dragon to sit on.

One of the concrete exterior's most distinctive features is the curvilinear entry canopy. The sculptural shapes of the walls and the canopy became a virtually liquid form. The canopy is actually framed in wood and lath and finished in troweled concrete, which received the same "sacked" texture as the concrete walls.

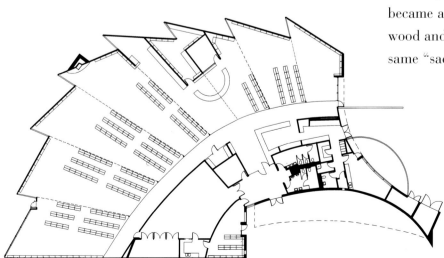

Previous Spread: *At night, the building's front facade appears like a friendly blue whale. Photo: Harvey Spector.* **Left:** *From the air, the building's sawtooth plan fans out across the site. Photo: Aerial Photography.* **Opposite Page:** *A tall concrete wall at the building's northwest corner anchors the front entry canopy.*

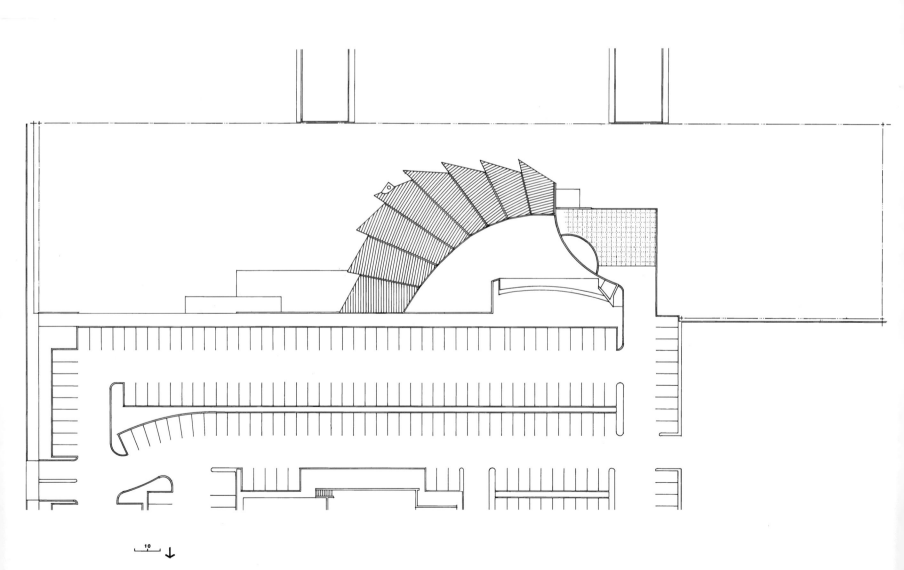

10

SITE PLAN

Above: *The southwest elevation of the library is a sculptural composition of concrete and shadow.* **Opposite Page:** *From the southeast, the library's sawtooth plan is readily recognizable. Photos: Harvey Spector*

45

Above Left: *The library's light-filled central corridor connects all of the reading areas and allows for art display.* **Above:** *A friendly dragon provides a welcome place to curl up with a book in the children's library.* **Left:** *Reading areas receive natural illumination from clerestory windows above.* **Opposite Page:** *The information area is found under one of the library's many clerestory windows. Photos: Harvey Spector*

Above: *East of the library is a garden with reflecting pool, defined by a slender con-crete wall.* **Opposite Page:** *The library entry features a central-pivot door and a warm wood ceiling. Photos: Harvey Spector*

Transportation District Maintenance Facility

Anaheim, California

This two-story bus maintenance building serves 250 buses within the local public transportation system. The building contains various shop facilities, storage areas, offices, and a lounge for the mechanics. There is also an operations building for dispatching drivers, containing offices, rest rooms, and employee lounges. Serving these two buildings is a two-story employee parking structure.

The design takes a no-nonsense approach to this humble program. The site is organized as a series of building blocks, juxtaposed at right angles. Square and rectangular openings underscore the buildings' rational planning and organization. Covered walkways frame views of the facility and provide welcomed respite from the hot California sun. The deeply recessed windows also shade the interior and help keep the building cool.

This public works project demanded low-maintenance, low-cost materials. Concrete block was used throughout the facility, both inside and outside, for its economy and quick erection. This virtually maintenance-free material is sandblasted to animate its surface and to render a high finish.

In citing this building for its design, an awards jury observed that it was "a practical solution for a practical problem. Pure and simple forms taking maximum advantage of shade and shadow create a pleasant piece of sculpture that works. It shows how a talented and experienced designer using simple materials can transform a very simple and often overlooked structure and make it into a very handsome part of the community. That's what architecture is all about."

Previous Spread: *The maintenance building's south elevation is a sculptural composition of concrete block.* **Above:** *A view of the bus wash area captures the bold rectilinear forms that dominate the facility's architecture.* **Opposite Page:** *The repetitive fenestration pattern of the bus-maintenance garage, viewed from the northwest corner of the operations building.*
Photos: Boyd/Connell

Above: *Durable, economical concrete block lends itself to the design's clean, geometric lines.* **Opposite Page:** *Glazed doors and high windows flood the interior of the maintenance garage with natural light. Photos: Boyd/Connell*

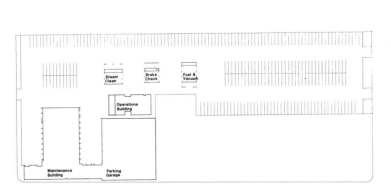

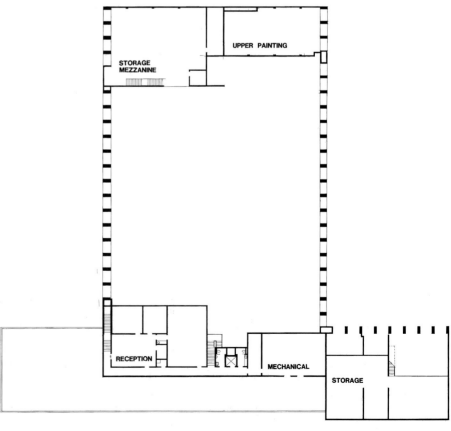

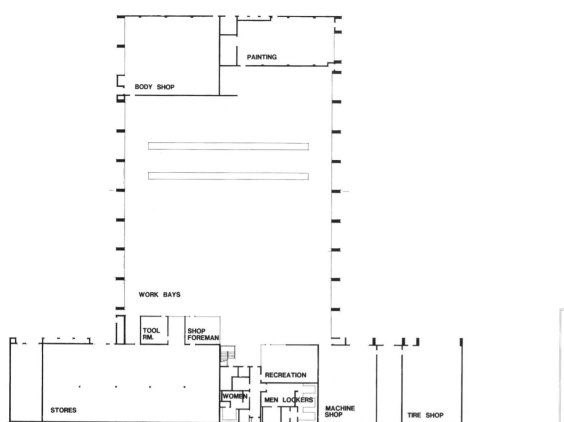

MAINTENANCE BUILDING FLOOR PLAN

OPERATIONS BUILDING FLOOR PLAN

Science Building
Polytechnic High School

Long Beach, California

The neighborhood that surrounds this 19,000-square-foot building is high-density, so the design had to work within a constricted site. Perhaps the most demanding program requirement was that the new building had to be built over an existing parking lot, because the 3,000-student high school simply had no vacant sites to build on. Thus, the first level of the building preserves surface parking, while the second and third levels contain laboratory classrooms and faculty spaces.

A current trend in high-school science facility design is to accommodate both lecture and labs in a larger room, which is served by class preparation areas and faculty offices. This arrangement works well in the Science Building, allowing prep and teacher areas to be shared. Three of the building's sixteen laboratories are devoted to chemistry, two are for physics, eight are for biology, and three are for physical science. The stairways connecting the three levels are contained in a dramatic three-story conservatory filled with greenery, which also serves as a backdrop to an adjacent lobby, conference area, and teachers' lounge.

The front facade of the building is a sheer plane of brick, with rectangular punched windows. Behind this facade is a muscular structure of concrete and steel. The steel frame of the laboratory spaces is painted dark green, in dramatic contrast to the robust, light-colored concrete columns. Smoothly finished concrete exterior stairs wrap the building at the front corners, allowing open-air circulation in this warm climate.

Previous Spread: *The slot at the building's center defines a zone where shared lab support areas are located in plan. Photo: Harvey Spector.* **Above:** *A dense neighborhood and a lack of other building sites required the school to be built over an existing parking lot. Photo: Eagle Aerial Photography*

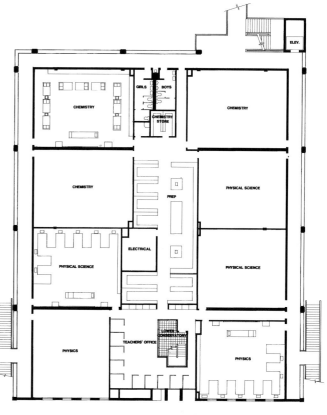

LOWER LEVEL

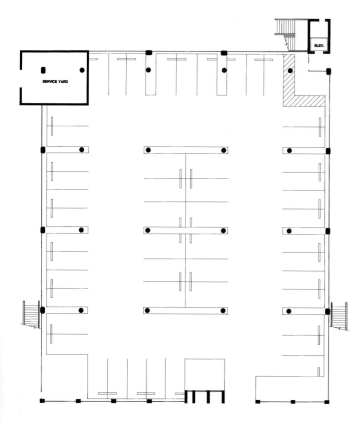

PARKING LEVEL

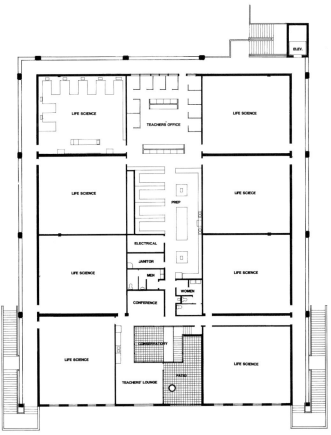

UPPER LEVEL

Below: *A model of the design expresses the billboard character of the front facade.*

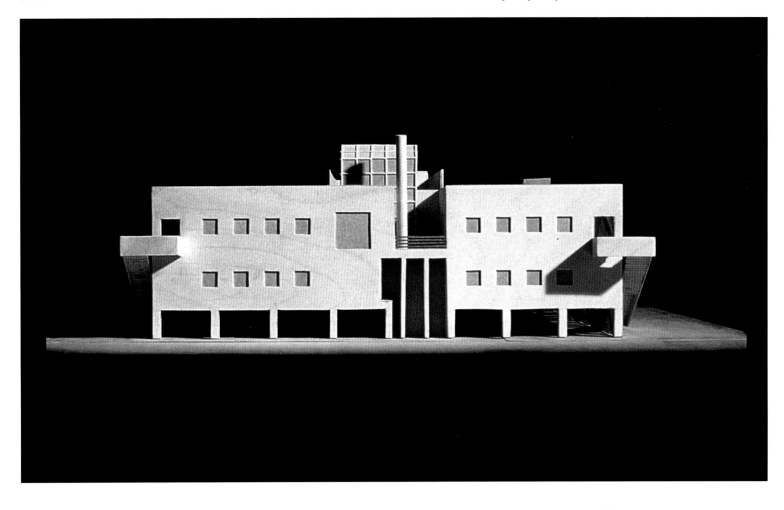

Above: *The lab wings are dark-painted steel structures supported with muscular, articulated concrete columns.* **Opposite Page:** *Concrete stairs wrap around the building's southeast and southwest corners, allowing open-air circulation. Photos: Harvey Spector*

Above: *A three-story conservatory is found adjacent to the teachers' lounge, conference area, and patio.* **Opposite Page:** *As viewed from the teachers' lounge, the conservatory is alive with light and greenery. Photos: Harvey Spector*

Orange County Law Library

Santa Ana, California

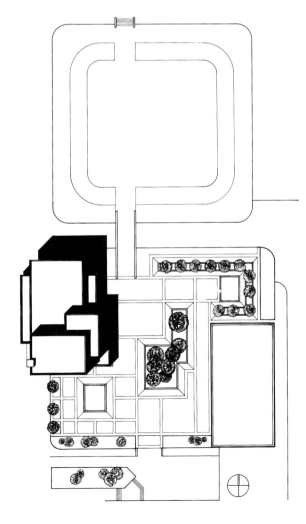

For use by attorneys as well as the general public, the Orange County Law Library occupies a site in Santa Ana's Civic Center, next to the central courthouse. The 30,000-square-foot building has one reading room, which makes the minimally staffed library easier to manage. Natural lighting is achieved with generous windows in the north wall of this space.

To communicate a sense of solidity and strength, not unlike the law profession itself, poured-in-place concrete was chosen as the building's primary material. The exterior features vertical reveals in the material (achieved with grooved plywood forms) to articulate the surface in the strong Southern California sun. To heighten the contrast, light-colored cements were used with white aggregate. The walls were then sandblasted to expose the white material.

Inside, exposed concrete was used for the pan ceilings, which needed no finishing and are maintenance-free. In the book storage area, concrete walls provide protection from the sun and allow storage against them. The building exploits the structural possibilities of reinforced concrete and a variety of finishing techniques. When citing this building for a design award, the jury wrote that it exhibits a "sophisticated use of concrete, with strong, handsome massing and consistent, sensitive detailing."

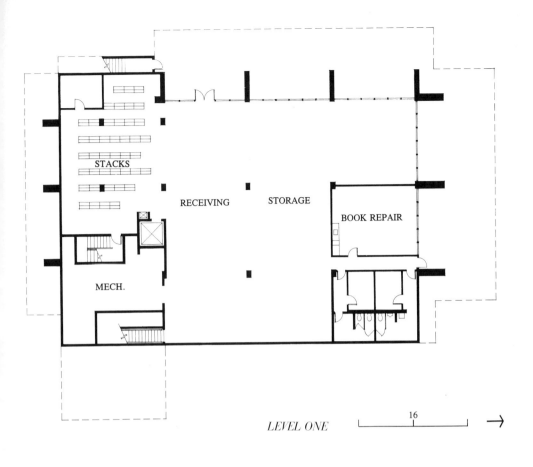

STACKS

RECEIVING   STORAGE

BOOK REPAIR

MECH.

LEVEL ONE

16

LEVEL ONE

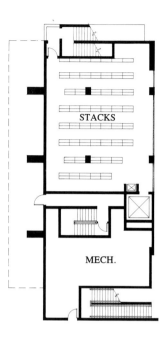

STACKS

MECH.

LEVEL TWO

COPY   TYPING   MICRO.

STACKS

READING ROOM

ASSIST.   LIBR   CONF.

LEVEL THREE

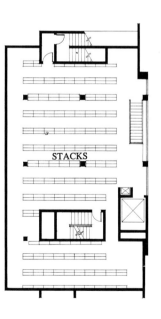

STACKS

LEVEL FOUR

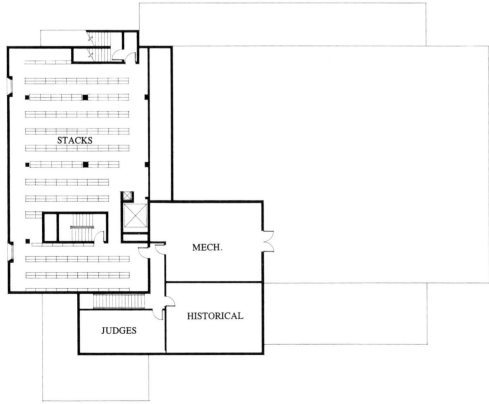

Previous Spread: *The library's north facade from the Court House reflecting pool.* **Above:** *The library's main entrance from the east communicates a sense of permanence through its concrete exterior. Photos: Julius Shulman*

STACKS

MECH.

HISTORICAL

JUDGES

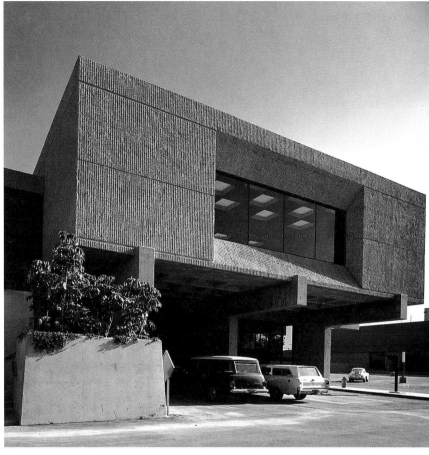

Above Left: *The book storage wing on the south side exhibits the variegated texture of the ribbed concrete.* **Above:** *The north wing of the library extends on a concrete structure over parking.* **Left:** *From the northeast, the library appears to be a collection of concrete forms, hovering over a fountain.* **Opposite Page:** *The library from the southeast corner, as it looks over the public plaza of the Civic Center.*
Photos: Julius Shulman

Above: *The library's main reading room is simply detailed, with overhead lighting incorporated into the concrete waffle slab.* **Opposite Page:** *The southwest corner of the library exhibits the sculptural qualities of concrete in its fire stair.*
Photos: Julius Shulman

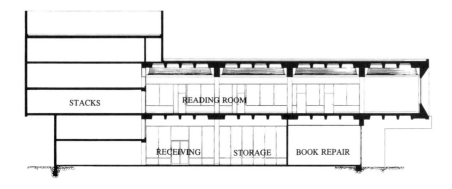

STACKS

READING ROOM

RECEIVING   STORAGE   BOOK REPAIR

Costa Mesa Library

Costa Mesa, California

Located in a park-like setting, the Costa Mesa Library is adjacent other civic landmarks, such as a community center, fire station, and a local historical commission. The 7,500-square-foot library houses over 45,000 volumes, and also includes offices, service areas, and a community room. The emphasis in the design was to provide a building that would serve the community. The requirements of the library staff were maximum flexibility and visibility.

The basic geometry of the library and its surrounding plaza is a series of circular structures and forms that interlock and overlap. The 650-square-foot community room is defined within the library as an interlocking circle, accessible after library hours through a separate entrance. The largest circular form encompasses the main reading room, administration, and book storage with a reinforced concrete tension-ring structure. The 116-foot-diameter ring supports the roof structure, allowing the interior to be column-free for maximum flexibility.

Exposed laminated wood beams span from the ring's perimeter to the center of the library space, and support a 12-foot-diameter skylight, which fills this space with natural illumination. A secondary concrete tension ring defines the lattice-shaded entry. A copper-coated galvanized iron roof and brick paving contrast with the concrete structure. The walls are cast-in-place board-formed concrete, which have a vertical texture and the imprint of the wood forms.

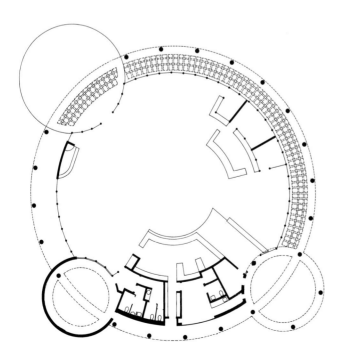

Previous Spread: *The library from the entry plaza with its fountain highlights the contrast between concrete and the warmth of the copper roof.* **Above:** *The front entry canopy is made of a concrete tension ring which supports a lattice structure for shade.* **Opposite Page:** *The concrete tension ring of the entry canopy intersects with that of the library, creating a confluence of geometry. Photos: Carlos Von Frankenberg*

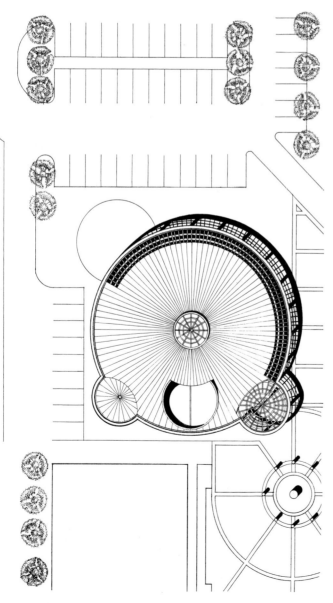

Above: *From the northeast, the library reveals the perforated roof that provides partial shading and shadow patterns.*
Opposite Page: *The library exterior, in this detail of the community-room wing, reveals the imprint of the wooden-form work in the concrete texture. Photos: Carlos Von Frankenberg*

SITE PLAN

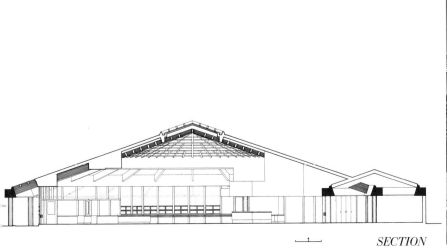

SECTION

Top: *The front entry canopy is made of a concrete tension ring, which supports a lattice structure for shade.* **Bottom:** *The library's southwest corner, where the concrete walls of the community room intersect the tension ring of the library.* **Opposite Page:** *The shading device over the library's windows filters natural light and protects against glare. Photos: Carlos Von Frankenberg*

Above: *The library interior is a single large space, with a lower ceiling over the circulation desk.* **Opposite Page:** *The timber roof structure dominates the interior, culminating in a 12-foot-diameter circular skylight. Photos: Carlos Von Frankenberg*

Fremont Elementary School

Santa Ana, California

This elementary school, designed for 800 students, was constricted on its two-and-a-half-acre site next to a 12-acre city park. To make the most out of the limited amount of space, and to merge the building with the landscape, the structure was recessed five feet into the ground, with earthen berms mounding up to the playground on the roof. This helps the building to conserve energy (because the earth is a good insulator) and it makes intelligent use of the land, providing a park-like setting in an otherwise crowded community. Recessing the building also made the building more earthquake resistant.

The plan of the school places open classroom areas at the center, with support spaces such as offices, lounges, and storage to the north. At the edges of the plan to the east and the west are found student restrooms, storage, and mechanical spaces. The flexible plan was accomplished with the use of a cast-in-place concrete structure. Concrete columns are spaced 30 to 40 feet apart, allowing ample reconfiguration of the spaces with moveable partitions. A three-foot concrete pan system was an economical choice for the ceiling, and allows light fixtures to be recessed into it.

The exterior is board-formed concrete, sandblasted to expose its white aggregate. This gives the concrete a stippled texture and lightens the color of the building. A jury that cited the school for a design award commented that the concrete is "a natural for a substructure outcropping like strata of rock."

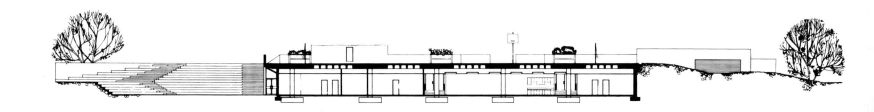

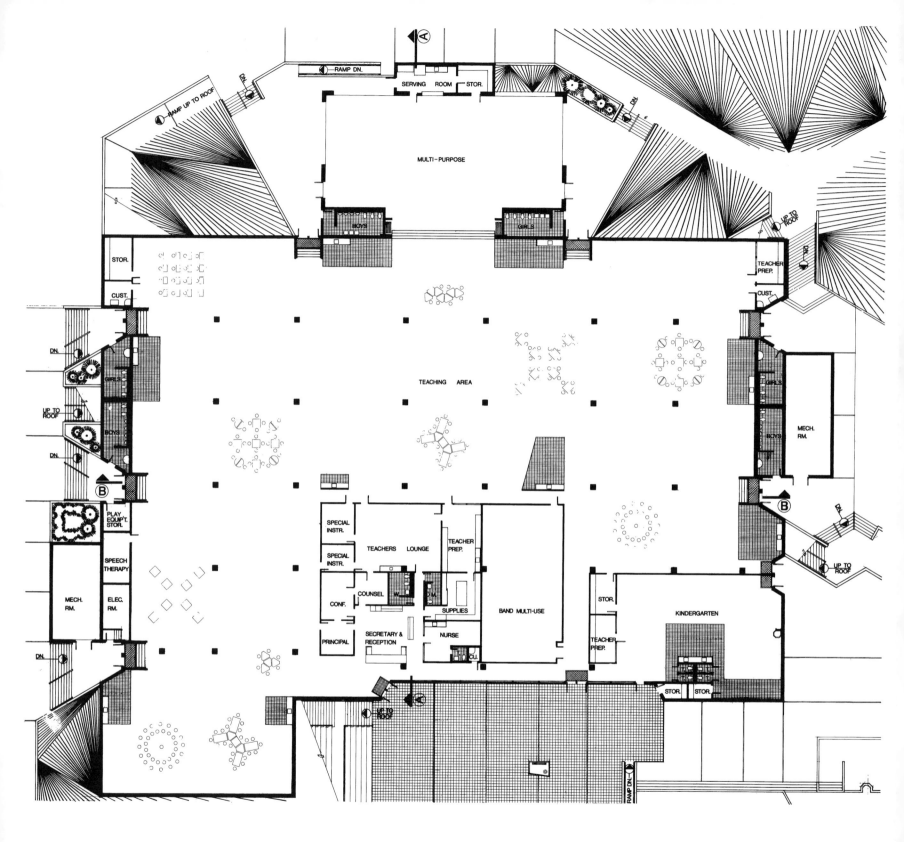

MULTI-PURPOSE

SERVING ROOM STOR.

RAMP DN.

RAMP UP TO ROOF

DN.

BOYS

GIRLS

UP TO ROOF

TEACHER PREP.

STOR.

CUST.

CUST.

TEACHING AREA

DN.

GIRLS

UP TO ROOF

BOYS

GIRLS

BOYS

MECH. RM.

DN.

PLAY EQUIPT. STOR.

UP TO ROOF

SPECIAL INSTR.

SPECIAL INSTR.

TEACHERS LOUNGE

TEACHER PREP.

SPEECH THERAPY

MECH. RM.

ELEC. RM.

CONF.

COUNSEL

SUPPLIES

BAND MULTI-USE

STOR.

KINDERGARTEN

PRINCIPAL

SECRETARY & RECEPTION

NURSE

TEACHER PREP.

DN.

C.U.

STOR.

STOR.

UP TO ROOF

RAMP DN.

SITE PLAN

Previous Spread: *Earth berms are used around the building for improved insulation and for better earthquake resistance.* **Opposite Page:** *The assembly area in front of the entrance provides a protected space with ample seating. Photos: Carlos Von Frankenberg*

Above: *The northwest corner of the school sports built-in play areas made of durable concrete. Photo: Carlos Von Frankenberg.* **Opposite Page Top:** *The concrete pan ceiling in the classrooms is expressed by a checkerboard pattern of lights and panels. Photo: Julius Shulman.* **Opposite Page Bottom:** *Super graphics are included on the otherwise unfinished interior concrete walls. Photo: Carlos Von Frankenberg*

Murrieta Valley High School

Murrieta, California

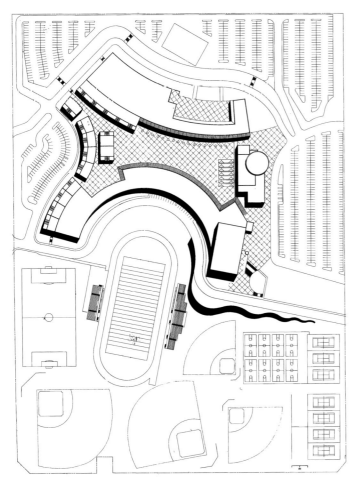

Designed for 2,400 students, the school is located on a 40-acre site. The imposing, curved facade was inspired by the Royal Crescent in Bath, England, of the nineteenth century, with which it shares a dramatic entry. The welcoming facade is further refined with the placement of track and football fields in front of it, providing the entry with a lush green landscape in the foreground.

The curve of the building responds to a running track, but its shape and size are identical to that of the Royal Crescent. Another allusion to the Bath building is the concrete and steel columns that march along the school's front facade, much like those at the Crescent. The school's columns support a latticework that will eventually be covered with vegetation, providing the building a soft, green canopy.

The entry drive follows the curve of the main building with its formal repetition of windows and lattice, terminating beside a long serpentine wall. The fifteen-foot change in elevation from the front to the back of the school allows for separate levels of pedestrian and vehicular traffic. Spectator access to the athletic facilities is through a large sunken courtyard with a vaulted bridge.

The students have responded very favorably to the covered lunch area in the building's central courtyard. Dubbed "the wings," the sweeping steel forms provide shade from the hot sun and appear as a collection of sculptural forms. "Meet me at the wings" is, at Murrieta, the social invitation of choice.

Previous Spread: *The school's front facade is distinguished by a curved row of concrete columns supporting a steel trellis.* **Top:** *The "wings" lunch area is a popular social gathering space in the school's courtyard.* **Above:** *The art and vocational areas are protected from the sun by a canopy supported by slender columns.* **Opposite Page:** *The building's curved front facade is identical in size and radius to the Royal Crescent in Bath, England. Photos: Harvey Spector*

Previous Spread: *The performing-arts theater is expressed as a single concrete volume that floats above its foundation.* **Above:** *The performing-arts theater lobby is distinguished by a glistening chandelier.* **Opposite Page:** *The exterior geometry of the performing-arts theater is expressed inside by its ceiling element. Photos: Harvey Spector*

Left: *The ceiling of the teachers' lounge incorporates curved elements that suggest the building's geometry.*
Photo: Harvey Spector

Above: *The school's triple gym is supported by heavy steel trusses and receives ample natural lighting.*
Photo: Harvey Spector

Troop Training Facility

Coronado, California

Located at the Naval Amphibious Forces Training Base, this facility is dedicated to training personnel for amphibious operations. Among the building's major areas are a shop, classrooms, instructors' offices, and a command area. The noisy shop area is isolated on the lower level away from the classrooms, while the command area is found next to the classrooms and the instructor preparation area. These spaces are carefully zoned for the efficient functioning and security of the entire building.

Of primary concern was the quality of the educational environment. Because of a diverse curriculum, the classrooms must function simultaneously as single-instructor halls, multi-media laboratories, and equipment training areas. The circular plan is segmented into eight classroom "wedges" and bisected by a dramatic 10-foot-high vaulted corridor with a continuous skylight at its apex. Each of the classrooms is entered by way of this central corridor and receives natural light from windows that wrap the circular building.

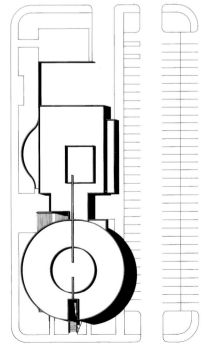

Concrete—both cast-in-place and block—was chosen for this building for its durability and low cost. The concrete breezeway functions simultaneously as a connector and a barrier between the building's four areas. The second story is cantilevered to accommodate the greater space requirement of the classrooms. Many of the facility's sinuous curves suggest ocean life-forms or the action of waves. The entire building is the result of a geometric system of planes, curves, and circular elements, whose exposed concrete and masonry construction make manifest its form.

Previous Spread: *The dramatic entry on the south side, via a concrete staircase, delivers one to the central corridor.* **Above:** *At the center of the circular wing, the main hallway allows easy access to all of the classrooms. Photos: Ronald Moore Photography*

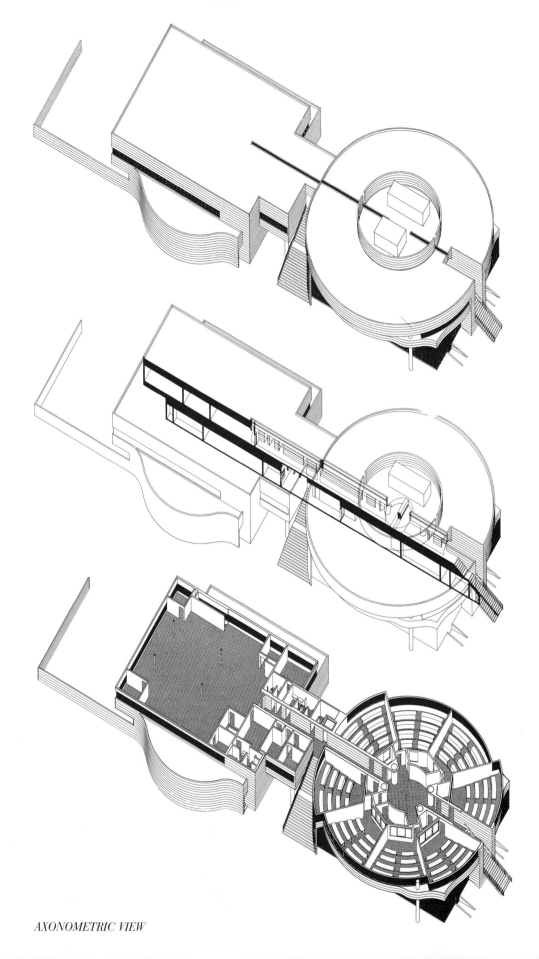

AXONOMETRIC VIEW

Above: *From the south, the building's curved concrete block elements are sculpted by the sun. Photo: Ronald Moore Photography*

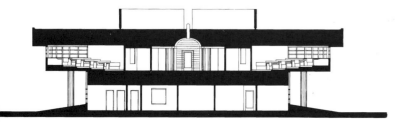

Above: *The south entry is distinguished by clean lines, achieved with the use of modular concrete block.* **Opposite Page:** *The curved stairway entrance on the building's south side as viewed from under the concrete waffle slab. Photo: Ronal Moore Photography.* **Following Spread:** *At the center of the circular wing, the main hallway allows easy access to all of the classrooms. Photo: Ronald Moore Photography*

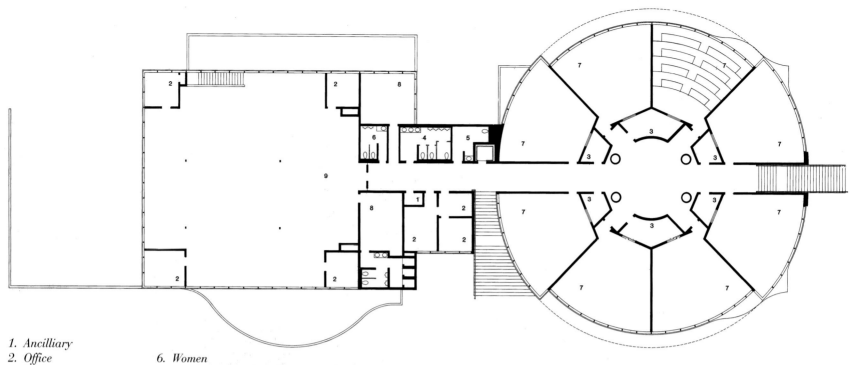

1. Ancilliary
2. Office
3. Projection Room
4. Enlisted Men
5. Enlisted Officers
6. Women
7. Classroom
8. Lounge
9. Branch Pool

SECOND FLOOR

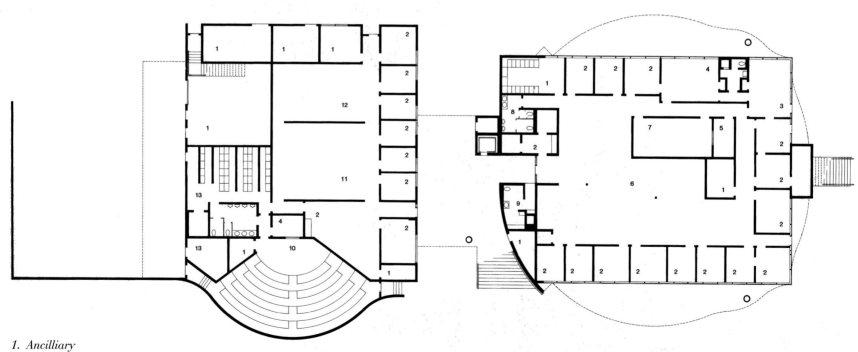

1. Ancilliary
2. Office
3. Commanding Officer
4. Chief of Staff
5. Projection Room
6. Headquarters Pool
7. Conference Room
8. Enlisted Men
9. Enlisted Officers
10. Classroom
11. Basic Amphibious
12. Reconnaissance
13. Locker Room

FIRST FLOOR

Underground City

Orange County, California

Cities exert a tremendous impact on the landscape, changing it forever. This Underground City for 20,000 would actually enhance the existing landscape, and hide the city beneath on a slope overlooking the Pacific Ocean.

The proposed plan calls for the construction of 5,000 units along a natural slope that rises to the peak of a hill approximately three miles away from the site. The units are a man-made concrete bluff along the shoreline, built in stages over a decade. In addition to single-family housing units there are shopping centers, a hospital, elderly housing, schools, restaurants, hotels, and an aquarium.

Approaching the Underground City from the Coast Highway, traffic travels underground, with no vehicles visible from the shoreline. An elevated walkway extends throughout the city, providing pedestrian access, and a second level of circulation accommodates bicycles. All traffic along the city's coastline moves via underground shuttle.

Tidal or current-action generators provide electricity directly from the ocean. Wave-action pumps deliver water to the top of the hill where desalinization takes place. Water released from large underground storage fields provides hydro-electric power at peak demand. Sewage treatment is done on-site in concealed facilities, with desalinated gray water recycled for irrigation.

Above the Underground City is a perfectly natural landscape, with views of the ocean. This green-space is used for vegetable gardens, parks, and recreation. Only from the water side is the Underground City visible.

Previous Spread, Opposite Page and Following Spread: *Drawings by Sergio O'Cadiz.* **Above:** *The Underground City would be constructed as stepped-concrete trays in the hillside, similar to the construction of Grandview Elementary School in Twin Peaks, California.*

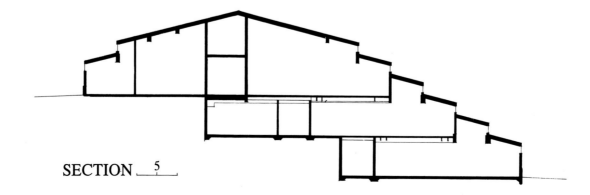

SECTION ⌐ 5 ¬

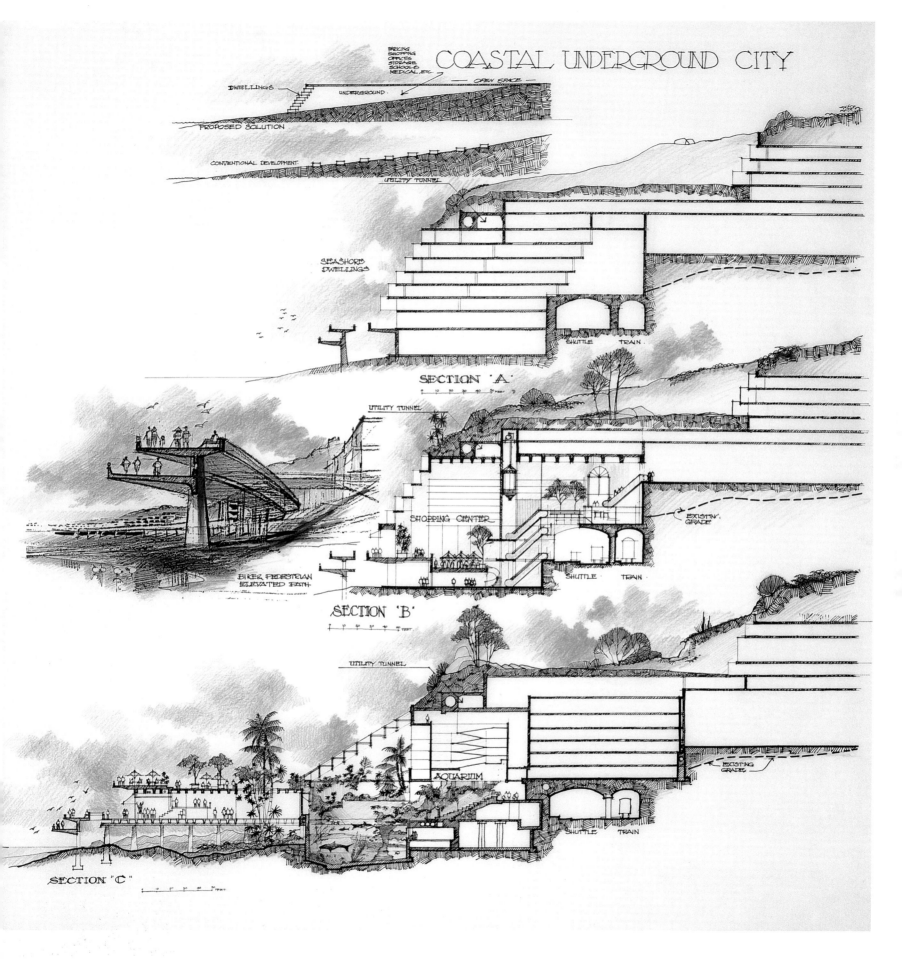

COASTAL UNDERGROUND CITY

PARKING
SHOPPING
OFFICES
STORAGE
SCHOOLS
MEDICAL, ETC.

DWELLINGS
UNDERGROUND
OPEN SPACE

PROPOSED SOLUTION

CONVENTIONAL DEVELOPMENT

UTILITY TUNNEL

SEASHORE
DWELLINGS

SHUTTLE TRAIN

SECTION 'A'

UTILITY TUNNEL

SHOPPING CENTER

EXISTING GRADE

BIKE & PEDESTRIAN
ELEVATED PATH

SHUTTLE TRAIN

SECTION 'B'

UTILITY TUNNEL

AQUARIUM

EXISTING GRADE

SHUTTLE TRAIN

SECTION "C"

Sergio
Cadiz
Moctezuma
.93

RALPH ALLEN HOUSE

Laguna Beach, California
1963

Designed to take advantage of the white-water view, this house is entered from above and steps down into larger volumes of living and family room space. Ralph Allen never lived in the house; it was a spec house and was sold upon completion.

CABRILLO PARK BUILDING
Santa Ana, California
1965

A simple, concrete-block park building, influenced by the Barcelona Pavilion of 1929. The four-inch-high block emphasizes the horizontal joint, resulting in a very inexpensive, sophisticated structure.

ORANGE COUNTY JUVENILE HALL EXTENSION
Orange, California
1966

The design doubled the size of the County Juvenile Hall, and included 117 sleeping rooms, 8 day rooms, 40 isolation rooms, and 9 classrooms. The structure consists of poured-in-place concrete with concrete block infill and a folded-plate roof covering the day rooms.

Photo: Julius Shulman

AUTOMOBILE CLUB OF SOUTHERN CALIFORNIA, BRANCH OFFICE
Garden Grove, California
1967

A simple rectangular structure, with large overhangs ringed by columns faced with white cement tiles designed by the architect. This was the first of many similar designs created for the Automobile Club and followed by other architects.

Photo: Julius Shulman

SANTA ANA FIRE TRAINING BUILDING

Santa Ana, California
1967

The "burning building" presented an opportunity for a very bold design. The program required a variety of shapes and windows for fire training exercises, which allowed the architect to build a piece of sculpture.

Award of Merit, Orange County AIA Chapter

PORTOLA PARK STRUCTURES

Santa Ana, California
1967

These buildings are similar to the Cabrillo Park Building: simple, low-maintenance structures.

ORANGE COUNTY LAW LIBRARY

Santa Ana, California
1972

This was the first library designed by the architect. A sculptural building with textured concrete, which employs natural lighting.

First Honor Award, Orange County AIA Chapter

Photo: Julius Shulman

ONTARIO CITY FIRE TRAINING CENTER
Ontario, California
1972

This poured-in-place concrete structure is appropriate for its use. In the classrooms, terraced seating with continuous counters and a rear-screen projection room provide an ideal teaching station. The students are close to the instructor for eye contact. This classroom is used in conjunction with the fire-burning building.

Photo: Julius Shulman

HUNTINGTON BEACH HIGH SCHOOL, DISTRICT GUIDANCE CENTER
Huntington Beach, California
1973

The building faces a busy street and is turned inward around a glass courtyard.

AUTOMOBILE CLUB OF SOUTHERN CALIFORNIA, ORANGE COUNTY HEADQUARTERS
Anaheim, California
1974

A two-story masonry building, very sculptural in appearance, featuring a cylindrical stairway.

Business and Industry Award, Los Angeles Beautiful

Photo: Julius Shulman

FREMONT ELEMENTARY SCHOOL
Santa Ana, California
1974

An understated, restrained, and effective site plan for maximum utilization. Concrete is used for a substructure outcropping like strata of rock.

National Energy Conservation Award, AIA/Owens-Corning Fiberglas Corp.
National Design Award, AIA/Concrete Reinforcing Steel Institute
Honorable Mention, Orange County AIA Chapter
Excellence in Electrical Design, Orange County National Electrical
Contractors Association Chapter
Photo: Carlos von Frankenberg

CYPRESS BRANCH LIBRARY, COUNTY OF ORANGE BRANCH
Cypress, California
1976

The library is a simple, rectangular building ringed by columns with a deep overhang. Allen followed the strong theme that had been established by William Periera in his design of previous city hall buildings.

Photo: Julius Shulman

RIO VISTA, JUAREZ PARKS
Anaheim, California
1976

The rugged concrete tilt-up proto-typical park building is appropriate to its use.

Photo: Robert Ward

U.S. POST OFFICE
Newport Beach, California
1977

A rectangular masonry building with a rhythm of deep recessed windows applied in a very orderly manner, creates a very functional, well-detailed building.

BANK OF AMERICA, DANA POINT BRANCH
Dana Point, California
1977

Clean, low-cost stucco building. Simple, yet functional and appropriate to its use.

MISSION VIEJO HIGH SCHOOL EXPANSION
Mission Viejo, California
1978

The school accommodates 400 additional students, and is a good neighbor to the original design. A simple solution to a very complicated program.

Photo: Julius Shulman

EL MODENA BRANCH LIBRARY

Orange, California
1978

A simple stucco building that features clerestory windows which conserve energy by reducing the artificial light levels during daytime hours.

Photo: Robert Ward, Sandra Williams Associates

ASSISTANCE LEAGUE DAYCARE CENTER

Santa Ana, California
1980

A concrete, block building, well detailed. It provides daylight through large north and clerestory windows. Large acoustically-treated covered walkways are in scale with the users.

Photo: Julius Shulman

ESCONDIDO MAIN LIBRARY

Escondido, California
1981

A two-story tile roof structure with light penetrating the roof through 36 clerestory windows. Light-actuated switches contribute to considerable conservation of energy during daylight hours. The bold shapes add a sculptural quality to the building.

Photo: Julius Shulman

ORANGE COVENANT CHURCH

Orange, California
1981

Unifying geometric forms that enable a construction of wholeness out of elemental parts.

Design Award Citation, AIA-Affiliated Interfaith Forum on Religion, Art, and Architecture

Photo: Julius Shulman

SMITH PARK POOL COMPLEX

Pico Rivera, California
1981

Designed with spirit, it looks vigorous, physical, and confident, as well as festive. It is a complete composition, integrated with the site and responsible about energy and budget.

Award of Merit, Orange County AIA Chapter

Photo: Julius Shulman

MacARTHUR INTERMEDIATE SCHOOL
Santa Ana Unified School District

Santa Ana, California
1982

A simple, concrete block structure. An oversized flagpole emphasizes that it is a school. A gold five-star cluster on a red background entry mural sets the tone for the school's namesake. The buildings are arranged around a large courtyard built one year in advance of the permanent, core consisting of an administration area, media center, science labs, multi-purpose room, kitchen, and shower and locker rooms.

Photo: Wayne Thom Associates

EASTSIDE POOL
Lancaster, California
1982

The simple, rectangular building houses a 25-meter pool surrounded by oversized, roll-up garage doors and 16 feet by 16 feet of rolling skylights, giving the opportunity of outside space with the push of a button. Roof-mounted solar collectors add to the conservation of energy. The structure is exposed on the exterior by large steel beams protected from the interior moisture of the pool.

Photo: Julius Shulman

RALPH ALLEN OFFICE BUILDING
Santa Ana, California
1982

A simple, five-foot modular mirrored-glass building featuring a 45-foot cantilever made possible by a 12-foot-deep truss running through the building. A sunken, brick-paved entry court provides an appropriate entrance for an architect's office.

ART & DESIGN CENTER
California State University, Northridge
Northridge, California
1983

A functional, direct, well-detailed building, capturing the spirit of Bauhaus. It provides a neutral and substantial background for creative activity.

Honorable Mention, Orange County AIA Chapter

TRANSPORTATION DISTRICT MAINTENANCE FACILITY
Orange County Transit District
Anaheim, California
1985

Deep overhangs protect large glass areas from sun, and supply natural light deep into the building interior. Bold shapes are used throughout the complex to provide aesthetic interest at a reasonable cost.

National Award of Excellence, AIA/National Concrete Masonry Association; Honor Award, AIA California Council/Regional Concrete Masonry Association; Honorable Mention, Orange County AIA Chapter State Concrete Industry Award, Portland Cement Association, Southwest Region; Photo: Jack Boyd

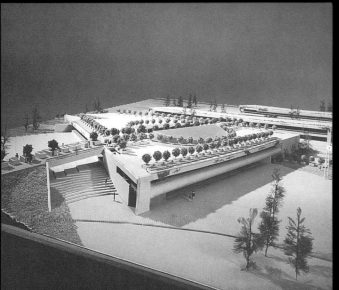

ORANGE COUNTY MASTER PLAN & PHASE I
Rancho Santiago Community College School District
Santa Ana, California
1985

These buildings were designed to fit into a residential neighborhood. A hillside approach was taken, with a one-story structure on the upper level and a two-story structure on the lower level. The space between these buildings is flat. This allows the buildings to cascade down the hillside in a natural way.

Photo: Julius Shulman

TROOP TRAINING FACILITY
Department of Defense, U.S. Navy
Coronado, California
1988

The design takes a corner and turns it with a circle. The exterior geometry features pleasant shapes, and the shape of the building relates symbolically to its use as an amphibious training facility.

National Award of Excellence, AIA/National Concrete Masonry Association; Award of Merit, AIA California Council/Regional Concretee Masonry Association; Award of Merit, Orange County AIA Chapter Photo: Ronald Moore Photography

COSTA MESA BRANCH LIBRARY

Costa Mesa, California
1988

A concrete tension ring provides a 116-foot clear-span structure with smaller tension rings for entry and classrooms, linked to the main tension ring like a daisy chain.

Photo: Ronald Moore Photography

CENTURY HIGH SCHOOL/Santa Ana Unified School District

Santa Ana, California
1989

The bold, concrete structure provides 300 parking spaces on the roof. Access to the roof is over a bridge with earth mounded in the front allowing a very organic appearance. The school is built around a large courtyard featuring three cantilevered flags—a shape used by Allen in other buildings. Particular attention was given to the shade patterns through the concrete latticed structures.

Concrete Building Award, Portland Cement Association
National Design Award, AIA/Concrete Reinforcing Steel Institute
Photo: Harvey Spector

JOHN F. KENNEDY ELEMENTARY SCHOOL

Santa Ana Unified School District
Santa Ana, California
1990

Two-story structure designed to fit into a residential neighborhood. The client dictated a romantic design approach. Large overhangs and a cantilevered lunch shelter add drama to the building.

Photo: Harvey Spector

KENNETH L. MOFFETT ELEMENTARY SCHOOL
Lennox Unified School District
Lennox, California
1990

This school is recessed into the ground with parking on the roof. A large amphitheater doubles as a main entrance to the building. Concrete was chosen to resist the retaining forces of the walls and weight of the cars on the roof.

Award of Merit, Orange County AIA Chapter
Award of Honor, Coalition for Adequate School Housing
Photo: Harvey Spector

FOUNTAIN VALLEY BRANCH LIBRARY
City of Fountain Valley
Fountain Valley, California
1990

A fan-shaped structure with light penetrating the roof throughout. One is drawn to the entrance by a sculptural overhang. The building is sited on the rear of a long, narrow site. A long, low wall with a reflecting pool adds a horizontal dimension.

Honorable Mention, Orange County AIA Chapter
Photo: Harvey Spector

GRANDVIEW ELEMENTARY SCHOOL
Twin Peaks, California
1992

The school is located in a mountainous area with hundreds of trees. The architect's solution was to locate the building on a slope between two flat areas, thereby making use of normally unbuildable land area. The building cascades down the hillside and has clerestory windows in all classrooms for natural lighting during daylight hours.

Photo: Harvey Spector

POLYTECHNIC HIGH SCHOOL SCIENCE BUILDING

Long Beach, California
1993

This building is located over an existing parking lot and is often referred to as a "space saver" school. The building fits beautifully into a tight space and evokes a powerful expression of structure.

Honor Award, Orange County AIA Chapter
Award of Merit, Cabrillo AIA Chapter

Photo: Harvey Spector

BUTLER INTERMEDIATE SCHOOL

Long Beach, California
1993

A two-story concrete structure with classrooms located in a staggered pattern which allows for windows on two walls. The school shares restrooms with the Park Department during summer and after-school hours. Adjacent to a community college, the concrete exterior fits in well with its surroundings.

Photo: Harvey Spector

MURRIETA VALLEY HIGH SCHOOL

Murrieta, California
1994

The school was designed around one curved end of the running track, resulting in a half circle the same size as the Royal Crescent in England. This is elevated 15 feet, which allows one to look out across the playing fields and over the countryside toward the mountains in the background. The colonnade trellis provides rhythm much like the columns at the Royal Crescent. The bleachers on the lower level are entered form a large sunken courtyard under a vaulted bridge.

Photo: Harvey Spector

RAIL RANCH ELEMENTARY SCHOOL
Murrieta, California
1994

The school is entered from a curved drive resulting in a quarter-circle core building containing multi-purpose spaces, administration, library, and two kindergarten classrooms. Additional classrooms contain pods of six classrooms located around a multi-use space.

BEATTY ELEMENTARY SCHOOL
Buena Park, California
1995

This is an addition to a large elementary school. Natural light enters the building through large clerestory windows and skylights, located in such a way that no direct sunlight hits windows that would otherwise cause heat to build up throughout the day. The maple chairs with spoke-like backs tie in with the ceiling grills for a dramatic effect.

Photo: Wayne Thom

ERIC BIRCH CONTINUATION HIGH SCHOOL
Fountain Valley, California
1995

Raised above the street, the entry to the school is well-defined as a singular opening in a long, sweeping curve of brick block. The brick wall, veiled in a lattice of vines, is used to evoke a feeling of permanence, referring to the ivy-covered schoolhouse of the nation's past. An outdoor amphitheater provides a natural meeting place for formal and informal use.

About the Architect

R alph Allen, the youngest of four siblings, was born in Nebraska during the depths of the Depression in 1932. Although from a family of sharecroppers, public education allowed him to excel. He was good at sports, but chose architecture as a profession because it sounded glamorous. He had little first-hand knowledge of the profession. To have indoor plumbing and a rug on the floor would have been a luxury. Architecture beyond this point was not too important to a high-school student in Malcom, Nebraska.

Allen entered the University of Nebraska and worked at night. He caught pneumonia and dropped out of school, and later went to work at a local dairy. He and his brother bought a semitractor and pulled freight after work at night between Lincoln and Omaha for his uncle.

After serving in the Navy during the Korean War, Allen returned to his architectural studies at the University of Nebraska. It was during this time that he realized that he had certain exceptional abilities, especially in the area of structures.

Upon graduating, Allen and his new wife went to California, where he worked for architect Thornton Able. He later formed an association with Gates Burrows, who needed a draftsman. Eventually they became partners, and began a series of projects for Orange County, one of the first of which was the Orange County Law Library, for which he won the first of his 12 design awards. He is a member of the College of Fellows of the American Institute of Architects, lives and practices in Santa Ana, California, and has a branch office in Chicago.